TOP TEN

Healing Stones of All Time

By Shelley Kaehr, Ph.D.

Top Ten Healing Stones of All Time
© 2009 Shelley Kaehr, Ph.D.

P.O. Box 234
Lewisville, TX 75067

ISBN: 0-9777556-9-X

Designed by Shelley Kaehr

Printed in the
United States of America

www.shelleykaehr.com

Also By Shelley Kaehr, Ph.D.

Gem Books:

Gemstone Journeys
Edgar Cayce's Guide to Gemstones,
Minerals, Metals & More
Lemurian Seeds: Hope for Humanity
Gemstone Enlightenment
Crystal Skull Consciousness
Divination of God:
Ancient Tool of Prophecy Revealed

Consciousness Books:

Lifestream: Journeys Into Past & Future Lives
Beyond Reality: Evidence of Parallel Universes
Explorations Beyond Reality:
Living Evolution Through Genetic Memory

Energy Healing Books:

Galactic Healing
Origins of Huna:
Secret Behind the Secret Science
Beyond Physical Reality:
Expanding Awareness Through Holographic
Mapping

Self-Help Books:

Just Write It! Step By Step Guide to Writing &
Publishing Your First Book
With This Ring: Making the Ultimate
Commitment to Yourself
Sales 101: Simple Solutions for Sales Success

Get author info and new releases:
www.shelleykaehr.com

Dedication

To my parents Mickey and Gail
who first taught me about stones

To Mark my brother & fiction cheerleader

To George Noory for inspiring the Top Ten
list for our *Coast to Coast AM* interview

To the late, great, Father Paul Keenan
for his friendship and inspiration

To the late Joe Crosson whose stone
is featured on the front cover

To Babzie, Geri, Mary Ann and Denny,
Pat & Paula, Linnea & Cindy...

And to all my readers and students who
support my work by purchasing my
stones and books...

I could not do any of this without you!

I Thank You All!

Contents

Foreword Thoughts by Dr. Shelley   7
Introduction   11
Why It's Important for You to Read This Book   11
     Earth Changes Are Real   20
On the Source of "Dis-ease"   21
     On Personal Responsibility   23
A Few Words on the Medical Establishment   29
     Stop Blaming Yourself!   31
PART ONE Energy Healing Fundamentals   33
One – On Frequencies and Energy   34
Sound in Gem Healing   36
     Entrainment   39
     Passive Healing   39
Color, Sound and Music in Gem Healing   40
Frequencies of Chakras in Hz   41
Chakras and the Stones of the Rays   42
How Color Changed My Life   46
Energy Bodies   47
     Physical   48
     Mental   49
     Emotional   49
     Spiritual   50
PART TWO - TOP TEN Countdown Revealed   51
10 - Rose Quartz   52
9 – Hematite   55
8- Amethyst   60
7 – Citrine   65
6- Aventurine   72
5 – Sodalite   75
4 – Lapis   78
3 – Fluorite   81
2 – Serpentine   85
1 - Bloodstone   88
PART THREE - Healing with Top Ten   93
Now What? How to Use Stones in Healing   94
     Self Healing   94
     Healing Others   96
Conclusion   98
Bibliography   104
About Shelley Kaehr, Ph.D.   108

***

"You have been telling the people that this is the Eleventh Hour, now you must go back and tell the people that this is the Hour. And there are things to be considered . . .
Where are you living?
What are you doing?
What are your relationships?
Are you in right relation?
Where is your water?
Know your garden.
It is time to speak your Truth.
Create your community.
Be good to each other.
And do not look outside yourself for the leader."

-Unknown Hopi Elder

Foreword Thoughts by Dr. Shelley

Once I read the memoir of Stephen King called *On Writing*. In it he spoke about writing as a form of interdimensional communication. As I pen these words, you dear reader, will not see them until some moment in the unforeseen future, so allow me to share a bit of what is going on in my world as I write...

It's late September, 2008, and I'm sitting here at 1:30 a.m. in a suburb of Dallas, Texas, typing on my computer which is sitting on top of what is normally my dining room table. My house is an absolute flurry of activity after a recent appearance on *Coast to Coast AM* with George Noory. I've got pounds of minerals lying around, piles and piles of them, along with paperwork, bags, shipping labels...all my healer friends who came to help me have gone home and I am

TOP TEN

reflecting on the day, taking a breath for the first time in hours.

I remember the first time I appeared on Coast years ago to discuss the healing properties of gems and I remember George telling me he'd never heard of this before, which was neat for me because he is probably one of the most open minded people alive who has surely seen and heard it all by now...

Since that first show, I've had the privilege to sell thousands of mineral specimens to people around the world and I've heard hundreds of stories about the incredible healings people received by simply carrying or wearing various kinds of minerals.

When preparing for my latest talk with George, I thought it would be fun to list a Top Ten in a kind of Letterman-like fashion. What I didn't expect was the incredible response to the stones – far greater than I'd ever received in the past.

When asked how I came up with this list, I picked stones that are both abundant and affordable, with energetic frequencies easily integrated by most people. The Top Ten are truly the most important stones of our time for mass consciousness.

These stones come from all parts of the world, primarily Brazil, but because they are limited, there is no telling how long we'll be able to tap these resources. I can only imagine the enormous interest in them must come from a deeper collective need on our part to connect with earth, to get grounded and centered in what is turning out to be some of the most challenging times in our history.

I've spent a lot of time these past few days thinking about why the public is reaching out for this information now. With all the change going on in the world, I believe energetic assistance is more critical than ever and the stones are destined to play an important part in our lives through the coming years.

There's a lot of talk about 2012 and the upcoming shift of the ages. I've long said I don't believe the earth will come to an end, I believe we'll go on personally, but clearly we can all recognize things shifting so fast and structures once stable collapsing before our very eyes. It can be scary to think about all the changes as we long to cling to the past, but something better always comes when we give up what we have. A brighter day is dawning and I believe these stones, the gifts of the mineral kingdom, can potentially be one of the many tools we need to assist us energetically at this time.

I said long ago I wanted to teach this material to people all over the world, and I suppose through my interviews over the last several years I have done exactly what I set out to do. As I told George, it isn't as much about the stones as it is about frequency and intention and learning to focus on what we want to achieve and create in our lives, knowing it is all within our grasp.

The stones you're about to read about are some of my favorites. I've been working with them and writing about them for so long they seem like old trusted friends to me, but to you they may be new. I hope you enjoy their companionship half as much as I do.

Shelley Kaehr, Ph.D.
September 2008

Introduction
Why It's Important for You to Read This Book

As we continue our journey together on the time stream, it is now February 2009. A lot has happened since I first penned my opening to this book and I would like to take a few moments to share my current passion about why this information is needed now more than ever in your life.

If you've been reading the papers, watching television or been alive and even remotely aware over the past several months, I'm sure I don't have to tell you things on our planet have seemingly started spiraling out of control.

The economy once considered the greatest in all the world is now crumbling, millions are losing their jobs and even the most optimistic people are beginning to panic.

TOP TEN

I have always been one to say the whole end of the world 2012 stuff was a big bunch of hooey, that we can change our reality by merely changing our consciousness, and I still believe that one hundred percent.

The reality is that in order to achieve what some would call the Thousand Years of Peace we will have to undergo some changes and I believe the collapse of certain sectors of our economy are a result of the change we must go through in order to reach a higher ground.

This isn't easy, I understand that, but if you can simply realize that all things come in cycles, then you can know that this too is merely a part of a cyclical experience we're having here on earth and it will all be okay.

Consider the ocean. There is an ebb and flow in the ocean. The tides crash on shore, then withdraw back into the depths of the sea. Life is like this and no matter how hard we want to buck up against mother nature and stop the ebb from happening, we simply cannot do that and not suffer. It is best to let go and let God, as they say. You are an infinite being and in the long haul, in the long history of your soul and your path here on earth, what's happening right now is minuscule compared to the grander scheme of things.

How could we as a society expect to continue with the rampant materialism and extravagant excesses we've been partaking in over the past twenty years or so? What comes around goes around and the piper has come for payment. That said, it is all in divine order!!! What have we learned about materialism these past several years? I'm sure many came here to get some really big lessons this time around and it is all as it should be. My only hope is that more people will begin to wake up and change their understanding of the world and what is going on here.

You and I need to be positive and that is becoming increasingly hard to do when so many are so panicked. What you think about expands and now more than ever, it is a great time to pray, meditate and become centered within yourself so you are emanating a peaceful vibration in the universe. The more of us who remain calm, focused and positive, the better things will be and the smoother we will go through this transition.

***

13

TOP TEN

Don't get me wrong, I am not in your shoes. Times are very hard, I understand that, AND you came here to have a spiritual experience and that is exactly what is happening.

Years ago I left a high paying corporate job after a long illness that thrust me on my spiritual path and let me tell you now, it wasn't easy. I had to learn how to do without many of the luxuries I'd grown used to and reprioritize things in my life.

When I see so many families struggling now, my heart goes out to them and on some level I understand the shock of not being able to do, to have and to be what you once were. It is a time to reevaluate your priorities and let go of the material overflow in your life.

When you think about it, what do you really NEED? Food, a roof over your head, love of family and friends and your health. Beyond that, seriously, you don't NEED a hundred pairs of shoes, suits, dresses and other excesses we have all enjoyed here. When you can learn to let all this extraneous stuff go, you will find a freedom and a peace there you have never known before. I know, I did it myself years ago.

I remember opening up my house one day and having a sale. People were walking out with my leather couch, hand carved dressers, television, appliances...it was one of the most liberating moments of my life to finally get the fact that I AM NOT MY STUFF! Wow! What a feeling!

Then on the path I was pretty much without material possessions for quite awhile until I began my rock business. Instead of filling my material world with the kinds of stuff normal people buy, I filled it with gemstones. I bought so many stones, you cannot even imagine it. I have owned much of what the gem and mineral world has to offer at one time or another in my life and I am grateful for that because it is how I learned about all these stones.

One day I was in my rock shop looking up at all the shelves and shelves of minerals and I had a sort of epiphany. I realized the rocks were weighing me down and I needed once again to purge, so I sold everything off. It took about two years to do it, but I did it, and then I spent 2007 writing fiction, which was one of the greatest gifts I ever gave myself.

TOP TEN

When *Coast to Coast AM* called me in the fall of 2008 to be on the show again, it was right before I was scheduled to take my full day gem workshop on the road with the Edgar Cayce Foundation. Trouble was, by the time these speaking engagements and radio interviews came about, I literally had next to no stones left in my house!

I had a dream about a friend who bought some of my stones and when I called her, she still had most of the pieces I sold her. She was going to open up a store but never did, and so incredibly, I bought them all back! It was both weird and exciting to see all my old stone friends again after a two year hiatus. They really do speak to me, seem to have personalities of sorts, so if you can imagine it was like going to a class reunion – a lot of joy.

Over the next month, many of the other material things I sold off or let go of also came back to me including my favorite piece of Larimar, the stunning golden calcite piece from the cover of my book *Gemstone Journeys*, and others. It just goes to show and proved to me once more that what is meant for you is coming whether you like it or not.

You probably heard that old adage if you love something set it free, if it returns to you it is yours, if not, it wasn't meant to be anyway.

When I wrote *Gemstone Journeys*, I talked about the fact that I titled the book because stones are like friends and they come into your life for a reason, season or a lifetime. In the case of my stone collection, I guess they needed a vacation from me, but then they came back after I had a dream...

So the point of telling you this is that these things that you think you cannot live without, I want you to remember it is only stuff and if you let it go, you will create a vacuum in the universe so you can receive more and if you let go of some things you love now, when the time is right, you can always get those again. The universe is a vast and unlimited space! We can create what we want and when you let go of stuff, you say to the universe, "I have faith I will have this again or something better!"

***

TOP TEN

What does all this have to do with Gem Healing?

Now I've gotten your attention, you might be wondering what in the world this all has to do with gem healing and why you need to read this book.

I feel an obligation to say something to you about all this simply because I am asked my opinions on it every time I lecture or give an interview these days. I want to share some of my personal story with you so that regardless of what is going on in your life at the future moment in time when you read this, it might offer you a glimmer of hope. I want you to feel the compassion I have for you now and feel like I am a friend who gets what you're going through, even when nobody else does.

I also want to reiterate why it is important for you to read on, learn about stones and other forms of vibrational medicine because these are the tools given to us all by Mother Nature to help us in acclimating to a planet that will continue to undergo more and more rapid changes as time progresses. Even in my polyanna-rose-colored-glasses view of the world, even I recognize shifts are happening and whether you consciously know it or not, you are feeling the effects of these shifts every single day.

More than ever with all the stuff hitting the proverbial fan, I need to get these ideas across to you BIG TIME because our planet is experiencing rapid shifts and changes and you need tools to help you make it through these interesting times.

Gems and minerals are some of the most prevalent, abundant and easy-to-use tools you can find to assist you.

***

TOP TEN

Earth Changes Are Real!

For the past several years New Agers have been warning everyone about the coming Earth Changes, but I am here to tell you this is no longer some woo-woo mumbo jumbo! Scientific evidence supports the fact that the magnetic frequencies around earth are shifting. Earth's heartbeat is slowing, the protective shields around the planet are diminishing and the overall vibrational frequency is increasing.

What in the world does that mean to you? The bottom line is that you and I are connected inextricably to the earth and it would be completely foolish to believe that when the earth changes its frequency that you and I are not affected. In reality, the exact opposite is true. We are influenced by the planets around us, as astrologers have said for thousands of years, and we are also influenced by the changes on our own planet.

Become aware of these changes and notice how you feel at any given moment. That is the first step to empowering yourself and controlling your destiny!

On the Source of "Dis-Ease"

They call it dis-ease for a reason – the body is not at ease. I believe all diseases are caused by the body's interruption in energetic frequency, meaning you simply have to shift your frequency somehow and health will be restored.

This is not always as easy as it sounds. There are deep energetic patterns in the human body we will look at later in this book. The causes of disease at a soul level are also very complex. In my way of thinking I believe on some level we choose illness as a way for our soul to grow and learn and when we discover the source of those lessons and the reasons we made those decisions, often we can let it all go.

***

TOP TEN

We are all connected inextricably by the web of collective consciousness and as such, we experience things in waves, masses of people often become afflicted by the same kind of diseases during certain periods of time.

For example, a decade ago we started seeing epidemic cases of diseases of the nervous system such as Parkinson's, Bells Palsy, Super Nuclear Palsy (which ended the actor Dudley Moore), Muscular Dystrophy and others.

Through the years I've been teaching energy healing, I've seen literal miracles occur with people who were shaking so bad they couldn't hold a cup of coffee and once they received energetic activations they suddenly stopped and could hold still again.

What this tells me is the person needs to let go, relax, allow the higher frequency energy to come through without trying to fight it and everything will be okay.

When cells are allowed to expand and relax, amazing things happen and the body heals itself by bringing more light and peace into the cells.

On Personal Responsibility

While I am inclined to believe that many of our illnesses are karmic, meaning we brought some stuff in from another life to work through, I believe these nervous system diseases are more frequency related and have more to do with the body's inability to function on the planet at this time.

Lately there are rampant cases of breast cancer and other cancer forms as well as the ever-present heart disease. Once the collective gets what it needs from these illnesses in ways of lessons and learning, I think occurrences of these diseases will lessen over time.

I don't want you to misunderstand where I'm coming from on this. I do not say this to blame you or anyone else for an illness, but you have to realize that in order to get well and let go of something, in my opinion, it is best done by assuming some sort of responsibility for it. If you were simply a victim, afflicted through no fault of your own, you would not have the proper focal point to give yourself "permission" to let it go and get well.

TOP TEN

What Happened...

I've been through this myself, believe me. I've talked about the fact I was quite ill many years ago.

I didn't want to discuss what it was because it is over and I don't want to give any energy to it. I have to admit on some level I must have been afraid to tell you about it, but I'm not anymore. For the very first time I am about to tell you what happened to me in hopes it might inspire you and help you on the path to your own healing.

I went to Costa Rica on one of my international exploits back in January 1994 with some friends from Canada. This was when the place was highly untamed and not a lot of touristas went there.

Despite my best efforts at avoiding illness, I got violently ill with a fever, etc. I remember I was staying in the home of the sweetest little family who owned a roadside diner and grocery store. The little mother came in to my room and was laying cold compresses on my forehead. She was so sweet!

She offered me a pill to take to help, but since I am always leery of any kind of ingested medications, I politely declined.

I now know that was probably a decision to alter the rest of my life! It might have helped me, but if it had, you and I would probably not be having this conversation some fifteen years later...it happens for a reason, you know!

That next month in February 2004 my friend was killed in the hiking accident I discussed in my book *Lifestream: Journeys Into Past & Future Lives*. I saw his spirit in the window of my house in March and I was thrown on my spiritual path at that moment.

Then in the summer of that year I began having symptoms of my jungle illness return and after a few trips to the doc, unsuccessful rounds of antibiotics, it was believed that a Central American parasite was literally eating me alive.

I weighed about 90 pounds at the time. To tell you how unreal that was, I am 5'4 and now weigh a healthy 115-120 depending on how much chocolate I eat! LOL!

Needless to say, I was a mess at 90 pounds. I looked like a skeleton. I was checked into the hospital and underwent a colonoscopy. Not a lot of fun, I can tell you that!

TOP TEN

Then the Clincher

I got well after the proper antibiotics were eventually prescribed, and basically forgot about this whole episode until the spring of 1997 when I started having unexplained pain and basically started not feeling well.

I went for months with this pain, going to doctors, nobody able to tell me what it was and it was getting worse by the week.

One day it was so bad I had to call my boss at the power company where I worked at the time and tell her I could not stand up. That's when a specialist was called in and I was eventually diagnosed with endometriosis, a reproductive disease too disgusting to get into here. If you're curious, look it up!

Normally people with endometriosis report chronic pain for years, but I can tell you I never felt a thing until that spring and by the time they found it in the fall of 2007 it was stage 4, really bad, and I had to have surgery. After a few unsuccessful drug treatments and a few surgeries, I finally had a hysterectomy in 1998 and got well immediately – physically, at least.

***

Miraculous Recovery?

One of the strangest aspects to my illness was the fact that everyone who came to see me in the hospital or while convalescing was convinced I was not going to make it. I mean literally people would come over and ask me point blank, "Are you going to die?"

I remember the first time I ever heard that. It was kind of like when you go to the office in your new sweater, feeling like you look great and a co-worker comes up and says, "Boy! You sure look exhausted today!" It is really a zinger for the old self-confidence, for sure!

I remember thinking about the question concerning my mortality for quite some time, then finally I said, "I don't know. I don't think so. I do plan to live."

There were many sleepless nights after that though, I wondered how I could possibly survive the grueling pain I was in. Thanks to this experience, I remain ever mindful to maintain a balanced state of health in my life, no matter what. I lived through illness once and I plan to stay healthy for the rest of my days.

***

TOP TEN

Strange Reception

After I got well, I moved from Texas to Colorado for a brief time and got going on my exercise routine, breathing fresh air and working on my health restoration, making it the number one priority in my life.

When I returned to Texas some time later, I was looking so healthy, so revitalized, people in the community who once saw me as knocking on death's door could not believe it was me, in fact they did not even recognize me a lot of times because my energy was so different, calm and relaxed as compared with the Type A who lived and worked there before.

I underwent an ego death of sorts. I had to reestablish new friendships, I kept a few of my old friends, but for the most part, people were scared of me. I don't think they understood what happened and how someone could go from being so weak and frail to so vital and alive.

I am living proof you can completely heal yourself from head to toe with time, faith and perseverance.

In a nutshell, that's how my journey into alternative therapies began. I wanted to know why this happened to me and how I could help others alleviate their own suffering.

A Few Words on the Medical Establishment

We cannot begin our journey into healing stones until I say a few words about modern allopathic medicine. Over the years, I've had a love-hate relationship with the medical establishment, as you might be aware of, if you've seen one of my lectures or read any of my books.

I used to falsely believe that when I was ill the medical establishment hadn't helped me, but I now see that was not true.

There is a time and a place for everything and I can tell you with great certainty, there were moments during my illness I would not have survived without the good ol' tried and true.

The problem isn't about *medicine*, it's about advertising.

TOP TEN

I'm sure I'm preaching to the choir here, but I find it absolutely appalling that we allow drug companies to advertise to consumers who know little or nothing about the inner-workings of their bodies.

Because of this advertising, our society is literally obsessed with rushing off to the doctor whenever we have the slightest ache or pain, wanting to tell the doc about how this pill we saw on TV is exactly what we need.

People tend to forget that sometimes our bodies feel discomfort for a reason and these things should not be masked, but with numerous medications and supplements swirling about our bodies, they often are.

My point here is that sometimes if you allow yourself to experience discomfort for a short time, you grow from it. When you feel the shifts of energy going on with the earth, the first instinct is to buck up against it, fight it and wish it away.

What I'm saying here is to instead relax, feel the pain or discomfort and imagine you can relax into the new energy and you will find you grow from the experience.

***

I believe allopathic medicine has a place for you and me. If you have a cut, for God's sake, stop the bleeding, in other words, go to the doctor!

As mentioned, I personally would not have survived my illness without the doctor and if you are ill, by all means, get treatment!

Stop Blaming Yourself!

Paradoxically, while I would like you to take responsibility for yourself and your illness and healing, I would also like you to stop blaming yourself for it. Let me explain...

There is a propensity in the New Age movement to blame ourselves when we are sick, and while I did say it helps to take responsibility for you healing, there is a big difference between that and simply beating yourself up over the fact you got that way in the first place.

I would venture to guess if you're reading this now, either you or someone you love has experienced illness, tragedy or both, and on some level, you are working through either how to heal this or how to help others. If this is you, then you need to hear my next story.

TOP TEN

I have a friend who was diagnosed and treated for breast cancer years ago. She had a mastectomy and was fine until recently when it came back on the other side. Some of our mutual friends were giving her a lecture about why she needed to take herbs and skip the medical treatments.

She spoke to me about it and wanted to know what I thought.

"What do *you* think about it?" I asked her.

"I believe it will save me."

That is all I needed to hear, "Then do it."

"You don't think I'm weak?"

"Of course not!" I said, "You would be weak not to follow your own intuition. If you believe this is what will save you, then it's true, and I'm all for it!"

I am happy to report she is doing better than ever now.

***

Need I remind you of the moral of this story?

Follow your instincts, keep your own counsel, do what it takes...you get the rest!

PART ONE

Energy Healing
Fundamentals

TOP TEN

On Frequencies and Energy

In all my prior books, I give you a brief discussion of how gem healing, or any healing, works. What you have to understand is you are not your physical body. Your body is the home for your spirit and too often in our busy lives we forget all about nurturing our spirit and concentrate on only what our allopathic doctor says we should do.

Once you've taken care of any pressing medical crisis and gotten yourself or your loved one back into a state of balance, that is when its time to take a deeper look into the hows and whys of the illness or dis- ease. There are alternative treatments you can use to assist the energetic frequencies in and around your body in becoming more harmonious with the planet as a whole.

As the earth changes, you are going to be affected. There is no way around it. Everything you see here in our physical world is nothing but energy so when one thing changes, it all changes.

In order for you to keep up with the changes you see in the world around you, the body needs more than what the traditional doctor can provide. You need what are known as *vibrational remedies*.

Gems are vibrational remedies because they are part of nature and have a certain purity and perfection to them. When you introduce the gem into your frequency, you begin to get into what I call energetic rapport with the stone and your frequency changes to match it. More on this as we go on...

Other vibrational remedies you may be aware of include essential oils, flower essences, and *sound*, which we'll look at next.

***

TOP TEN

Sound in Gem Healing

Believe it or not, sound plays an important role in all forms of healing, including the work you're going to be doing with gems and minerals.

An example would be if you were trying to tune your guitar. Let's say you needed to tune the strings by comparing the sound to the sound made by another instrument like a piano. You would play the piano note and strum your guitar. At first the guitar note would sound completely sour until you twisted the tuning keys and the note eventually sounded the same, or *resonated* with that of the piano.

Your body is the same. If you introduce a stone into your field, at first you might not feel a thing, or with some stones, you may feel energy that is so strong it feels strange. Then after a few minutes that feeling goes away and there is harmony between you and the stone. You "tuned in" to its frequency and by doing so, normally your frequency increases and the higher the frequency the more you are in a state of well being and peace within the physical body.

Another metaphor for how this works would be when you go into a room full of people who you don't know. At first if you're like most of us (including yours truly here) you may feel a little uncomfortable, out of place as you start to look around and see if there's anyone you know.

If you find a familiar face, you go up to them immediately. Why? Because they share a similar frequency to you and are familiar to you energetically. On the flip side, if you don't see anyone you know, you will continue to feel a bit out of place until you gravitate to a stranger, or them to you. Someone may speak to you at the buffet line, for example, and at first you may not know what to talk about except the weather, but soon you're talking and carrying on like old buddies. That's because you've tuned into them and they to you!

Without completely rehashing all I've said in my other books over the past several years, I share these metaphors with you to explain to you why I believe gem and mineral healing works by discussing sound.

***

TOP TEN

The universe was supposedly originally created by a single sound, the OM, which reverberated out into the ethers thus creating every single thing you and I see and take for granted on a daily basis.

You and I are literally made up of the same stuff as the chair we're sitting on, our desks, tables, plants, birds, animals and yes, gems. We are all a part of this big cosmic vibrational creation called life and if we want to experience this planet with ease, we must find a way to come into a state of harmony with all the things around us in the natural world.

In my seminars, I tell people the reason this works is because you are vibrating at a certain frequency and the stones are vibrating at another frequency. When you put the stones on your body either by wearing them in jewelry, placing them on the body or holding them in your hand, pocket or purse, you introduce that frequency into your own and you begin to shift to match the waves emitted by your stone. I call it getting into rapport with the stone.

Another term for this phenomenon widely used in sound healing is *entrainment.*

Entrainment occurs when the vibration of one object shifts to that of another. I was first shown this by a Shaman many years ago, and since then, I have personally witnessed many miracles regarding gems and stones and believe it to be one of the most powerful and prevalent tools we have at our disposal for creating positive and lasting change in our lives because the stones assist us in shifting our frequencies to theirs and thus create shifts in our consciousness.

When we shift our frequency, reality shifts instantly. Sound can facilitate that, so can stones.

Passive Healing

Stones and minerals have beneficial frequencies. When we work with them by simply placing them in pocket or purse, holding or wearing them as jewelry, we take advantage of a relatively passive form of healing, meaning it does the work for us by simply allowing it to be, shifting our frequencies gently and pervasively.

It seems like I am repeating myself here, but they key to understanding why any healing works is because of entrainment. Minerals help you by simply being in your presence. Period.

TOP TEN

Color, Sound & Music in Gem Healing

Because all matter is originally created by sound, each sound resonates with colors of the spectrum, and each correlates to notes on a musical scale as is shown on the diagram below.

Note	Chakra	Color	High Note
C	Root	Red	E
D	Sacral	Orange	F#
E	Solar Plexus	Yellow	G#
F	Heart	Green	A
G	Throat	Blue	B
A	Third Eye	Indigo	C#
B	Crown	Violet	D#

Likewise, gems and stones also resonate with colors in the rainbow spectrum and notes on a musical scale. More on that in a moment...

***

Shelley Kaehr, Ph.D.

Frequencies of Chakras in Hz

7th	Crown	172.06 Hz
6th	Third Eye	221.23 Hz
5th	Throat	141.27 Hz
4th	Heart	136.10 Hz
3rd	Solar Plexus	126.22 Hz
2nd	Sacral	210.42 Hz
1st	Root	194.18 Hz

I have finally researched the exact Hz frequencies for our seven chakra centers. This page is dedicated to the dozens who have asked over the years. Enjoy!

TOP TEN

Chakras & Stones of the Rays

Speaking of color, one way you can use color in healing is through the stones and I wanted to provide you with the colors here because I think this information is good to know, although many of these stones are not in the top ten because they are not always as easy to get or as affordable.

Chakras are explained in great detail in my other books. They are the seven energy centers within the body.

If you could see these, they start at the base of the spine and go up to the center of the top of your head.

Crown – White – Crystal

Crown center is located at the top of your head, and is associated with connecting you to your source, or higher power. It's white and the plain quartz crystal is the stone to open this center for you.

When you think of source, you could equate it to the power supply for your body. As your computer or TV has a power cord, the energy supply for our energy body comes from above and what better stone to use for that than the data transmitting clear crystal – the same stone used to power up many of our electronic devices.

Third Eye – Purple - Amethyst

We will discuss Amethyst later in the Top Ten, but for now I will say that it is vibrating at the same frequency as purple ray so it opens up your third eye center which is located in the middle of your forehead.

Third eye is associated with the kinds of information we cannot get through the normal five senses. It is ESP, extra sensory, and when you work with this stone, you will be assisted in opening yourself up to receiving more information than ever before.

Throat - Blue – Sapphire

I went to India a few years ago and bought myself a beautiful blue sapphire ring. I love this stone and it is blue sapphire (there are actually many colors of this stone ranging from yellow, to pink and even brown) that is vibrating at the frequency of the blue ray. Not only is blue the ray that opens up the throat and assists you in communication, it also promotes calm relaxing energy and peace.

Blue is also associated with water and emotional healing. It will ease a troubled or broken heart and put it on the mend.

TOP TEN

Heart – Green – Emerald

Emerald is vibrating to the tune of the color green and that is the color of healing and opening the heart, which is a mighty difficult task for many of us. Any difficult emotional state will be relieved by this color as well as heart healing of any kind.

Solar Plexus – Yellow – Citrine

Citrine is one of the Top Ten and it vibrates in alignment with the yellow ray which strengthens our resolve and personal power. Yellow is the color of planet Jupiter which brings luck and prosperity so if you need more serendipity in your life, use this color to bring courage and abundance to any situation.

Sacral – Orange – Carnelian

Orange ray is expressed in the mineral world through carnelian which is a form of agate. This stone was often carved into signet rings in the ancient world and leaders such as Napoleon were said to have worn this stone into battles for protection.

The orange ray is also about creativity and your ability to create anything you wish in your life be it art, work or money.

Root – Red – Ruby

Ruby is a cousin to the sapphire. Chemically the two stones are nearly the same. Ruby is the red ray which opens your root chakra center, and grounding you, connecting you to the earth. As I mentioned earlier you must be connected to source energy through the crown in order to be balanced, you must also be simultaneously connected to earth. As above, so below...

Red assists you in being here on our planet so you can thrive and do your work. A few years ago after I bought my house, I was guided to put lots of red and gold colors in it. At first, it brought up a lot of my issues about being grounded after living in the ethers with purples and blues for many years.

Now I find it nurturing and grounding and gain a lot of energy from my home, a concept I thought I would never discover given my love of travel and adventure.

***

TOP TEN

How Color Changed My Life

With time and patience, I found the more grounding colors of red and orange brought me great peace once I began to fully understand how I could create the tone for a space simply by painting it.

My house still has some purple rooms for more ethereal pursuits, a sky blue room for rest and relaxation, daydreaming and creativity, and the gold room with red accents I once hated now assists me in creating and completing more writing endeavors. Each space I created has a time and a place for me and I find I can completely shift my energy just by stepping into the different rooms of the house. Why? Because the color frequencies are bouncing off the walls, interact with my energy and I become entrained with the frequency.

Gemstones and the Stones of the Rays will further enhance your experience of color. If you need to create certain things in your life, use the corresponding stone by wearing it, keeping it in your home or office and watch what happens!

Experiment with color and see for yourself how it can change your life!

Energy Bodies

You are not physical. The body you see in the mirror day in and day out is an illusion. Period. If you could see yourself how you really are, you would notice yourself as infinite energy fields, connected with everything else here on earth and beyond.

To teach this is often difficult so I like to talk about the fact that your field has different densities or thicknesses to it, depending on proximity to the body.

In prior books, I've described three layers to the field. Here, I am guided to break this down into four distinct fields.

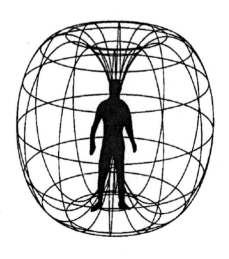

TOP TEN

Physical

This is the field closest to the body that holds your physical well-being. When I place my palms over a client, for example, there is a very thick energy field that is literally an inch away from the body.

You can feel this on yourself by running your hands an inch over your torso or try this with a friend. You will see what I mean.

When there are blockages in this field, you are more likely to become sick, which is why this is, on some level, the most important field around your body.

We've talked all about medicine already so I won't repeat myself, but I want you to understand that before that illness became present in your 3D mind, it was originally a thought, a piece of stuck energy in that field closest to you.

In order to prevent illness and that trip to the doc altogether, you need remedies and work being done to ensure your field is enlivened closest to your body.

When you move that energy, get your chi going again, illness will move away and wellness will be restored once more.

Mental

This is the part of your field that is two to three inches from the physical body. Here is the layer where ego lives, that part of you who thinks you are a physical person. It has to do with your personality and interests, habits, both good and bad, and karma. It is the *conscious mind.*

If prosperity is a problem, this is where the energetic component to the situation lies. Remove it by working with this field, stirring up the energy, and watch how abundance comes flowing in.

Emotional

While I used to clump both mental and emotional into one category, I am guided to change that for this book. Your emotional body represents a higher form of *subconscious* spiritual energy. It's how you feel in response to the world around you, the *subconscious mind* I speak of in my hypnotherapy books.

Past memories, both joyful and sad, things you remember fondly and things you resent are all energetically happening here in your emotional body, which is found about four to five inches above and around your physical body.

TOP TEN

Spiritual

This is the field that connects you with your Creator or higher power. It normally begins about a foot from the physical body and encompasses that which connects you to all else in the universe.

Here is the field where you store life lessons, reasons you came to being, why you're here and all the bigger picture endeavors in life that remind you why you are a spiritual creature in the unified field.

We all have an inner voice or knowing, yet often we hesitate to use it or don't trust our own inner guidance.

Work on this farthest layer of your field will allow divine guidance to come through you more readily. When we are able to finally learn to listen and follow that highest level help, our lives instantly become magical and problems that may have once plagued us seem to disappear.

FOOD FOR THOUGHT
Did you know many women's cosmetics already feature the beauty-enhancing, wrinkle reducing rose quartz?

PART TWO

TOP TEN
Countdown Revealed

TOP TEN

10 – Rose Quartz

Chemical Composition: SiO_2
Located In: Brazil & worldwide
Metaphysical Properties:
Assists with loving others, self -love,
compassion and universal love
Physical Healing: strengthens heart,
weight loss; wrinkles

We begin our countdown with
Rose Quartz, one of the most common
and most profound minerals on earth.
It is a silicon-based member of the
quartz family. Later we'll talk more
about why that is so important.

The quartz family is incredibly
large. Clear quartz has one frequency
but when trace amounts of titanium
are added, the result is the beautiful
pink crackly stone known for its ability
to open our heart centers to love and
peace.

On a physical healing level, Rose Quartz can assist you with any heart related ailment, its high frequency shakes loose lower vibrations leaving you feeling peaceful and at rest.

The frequency has also been known to assist people with weight loss and can also remove wrinkles and signs of aging which is caused by stress in our lives.

I name Rose Quartz as one of the top ten because it is a common stone with beneficial frequencies for a large number of people. Also physically and spiritually, opening our hearts is one of the biggest challenges facing mankind as a whole. Physical heart problems continue to plague society and our current level of emotional disconnect with our fellow humanity seems at epidemic proportions.

I personally believe this is due at least in part, to our advances in technology. As we become more and more connected by electronic devices, these things are making face to face contact less and less prevalent, thus we are isolating ourselves in cocoons rather than interacting with each other. Ultimately, we become isolated and the heart center suffers.

TOP TEN

I've been hearing a lot lately about this new Wii game. Everyone at my gym is raving about the incredible level of virtual technology this game has and the fact that you really feel like you are playing tennis, boxing, etc., however you are not actually doing it, because the journey is all in the mind. While this is a neat metaphor for how we create things with our minds, it also exemplifies the way modern society is going. We have so many incredible tools at our disposal we can become friends with an imaginary team mate on a virtual game rather than actually going outside on the real tennis court, etc. It is quite Orwellian, in my opinion. It seems we are headed for a life not too far removed of that of George Jetson and his fictitious space family...I hope not!

Rose Quartz is coming in as an important energetic support system at this time to open ourselves to actually getting out, conversing with *real live* human beings through innerpersonal relationships and learning how to love in the physical world once again.

***

FOOD FOR THOUGHT

Did you know giving blood is good for men's health? Its's true! Women rid their bodies of excess iron during monthly cycles, but men need to give blood in order to balance blood iron levels to maintain good health. Hematite is the ore of iron.

9 – Hematite

Chemical Composition: Fe_2O_3
Located In: Brazil, Minnesota, USA
Metaphysical Properties: Takes on negative or unproductive energy, offers psychic protection, grounding
Physical Healing: reduces fever, assists with circulation due to magnetic attributes

When people write to me and tell me their life is going to heck in a hand basket, chaos is spinning them out of control and they wonder how to get out of it, I tell them to turn to one of my favorite stones, Hematite.

From the Greek word *haimatites* meaning "blood-like," this stone is truly magical. It is naturally magnetic iron ore and for that reason, it draws excess or negative energies into it so you don't have to deal with them.

TOP TEN

I've seen Hematite do its thing dozens upon dozens of times through the years. Jobless people carry it in their pocket only to find it cracks within a few hours, my own necklace broke and fell to the ground, the inexpensive five dollar rings you see in the stores crack under pressure so you won't have to...It is truly amazing.

Magnet therapy is big now and with good reason. It stirs the circulation, gets the blood moving and hematite does all this too, only for a fraction of the cost.

Hematite works the same way as a magnet, and as such, pulls energy into it that may or may not be detrimental to you. For that reason, if you have stress on the job or elsewhere in your life, when things seem to be spinning out of control for you, Hematite is a wonderful stone to use.

I believe one of the biggest problems we face today is the fact that we are more sensitive to the energies of others than we might imagine. Certainly one of my big epiphanies in life was the day I discovered that I am often so sensitive to other people I will actually take on and act out their stuff!

Shelley Kaehr, Ph.D.

Through the years I've learned how to shield myself, temper that from happening, and the stones have been a big help to me personally in this area. What I've found from working with thousands of people in counseling, is that I am not alone. Many of us are being affected by the world at large, and while I believe it is true that 'we are all one,' and that can be a good thing as we learn to work with others and assist our fellow man, I also believe when things aren't going so well or there is turmoil in our midst, we can become negatively impacted by this energy and it can ultimately lead to dis-ease.

If this sounds like you, there are all sorts of mental exercises you can use to shield yourself from these energies. You can bring white light around yourself, evoke a violet flame, or you can simply use the vibrational frequencies of stones like Hematite to assist you in keeping your energy to yourself, so to speak.

I always like to use the example of the shopping mall.

I'm personally not a big fan of shopping. When I go, I try to think of exactly what I need and the way to get in and get out in the least amount of time because I find the mall to be draining on the energy. When you arrive at the store, you may feel energized, but often by the time you get home, you feel like going to bed or taking a nap. I believe that is because the energy of so many people around you has an affect, takes its toll and wears down the energy field.

Hematite is on my Top Ten list because in my opinion it is the very best stone to use when you need to function in the world without picking up on all the stuff floating around in the ether. When you wear it in a necklace or ring, or carry it in your pocket, rather than you personally being afflicted by various energies, be they good or bad, the stone absorbs all the excess you can't handle and serves as a buffer between you and humanity.

It is also helpful for the throat to clear the old energy from the Piscean Age away so you may speak your truth freely and finally say what needs to be said.

In healing, I always like to use lots of Hematite around someone like you would use magnet therapy. If you are offering healing to others (which will be discussed later in the book) you can put Hematite pieces all over and around the body with the intention of getting the circulation going, and moving and balancing the chi. It works wonders!

The Greek reference to Hematite's blood-like qualities refers both to its ability to temper high blood pressure and to the fact that when it is not in the big round dark silver shiny pieces, Hematite appears in many other minerals as dark reddish brown streaks. Why? Because iron is a common element on our planet and it can be found in many minerals.

Right now with all the changes bombarding us in this New Age and as we get closer and closer to the 2012 reality and the new life unfolding for us, I feel Hematite has come in to assist us in keeping focus and grounded as possible while continuing to undergo earth changes at warp speed.

FOOD FOR THOUGHT

Most of these stones in TOP TEN are found throughout the world, which is why they were chosen. I list a few of the most common places where deposits are found around the world for your information.

TOP TEN

8 – Amethyst

Chemical Composition: SiO2
Located In: Brazil, Uruguay, Colorado
Metaphysical Properties: opens up
intuition and psychic gifts, aids
alcoholism; assists in tempering
addictions, calms the spirit
Physical Healing: headache relief

     Amethyst is a dark purple
member of the quartz family that gets
its color from iron. It is vibrating at
the same frequency as the violet or
purple ray, as mentioned in the stones
of the rays section, which is why it is
used to open the crown chakra center
and the third eye center.
     On the rainbow spectrum, violet
is a higher frequency with shorter
waves so this stone is good for
removing any kind of energy block
and opening your mind and spirit to
the universal mind.

Amethyst also helps those suffering from addictions, particularly alcohol addictions because of the lore surrounding it. In Greek mythology, Amethyst was an innocent girl on her way to pay homage to the Goddess Diana when the wrathful Bacchus, god of wine and libation, decided to inadvertently turn her into a stone. When Diana chastised him for his rude behavior, he cried his big purple tears on the girl and turned her into the lovely stone Amethyst. Now she assists anyone who indulges too much.

If you find yourself suddenly thrust on the spiritual path, you will likely be drawn to Amethyst, at least for awhile. It assists you in seeing the broader vision of things and attuning yourself to the unseen world.

Amethyst will assist you in washing away the old and opening your energy field so you can move into higher states of being where you operate from your intuition rather than the more three-dimensional rational mind and you use the intuition to take action and make decisions.

***

TOP TEN

When I mention the fact that Amethyst is a tool for overcoming addictions, I mean this stone can assist you in breaking any habit you wish to remove from your reality by doing a kind of pattern interrupt so you will break free of whatever is holding you down. It helps you gently release any way of life, person or behavior you must let go.

The truth is the entire society thrives on addictions of various types. When we think of addiction, normally alcohol or drugs come to mind, but these days, with all the television programs, junk foods and other unhealthy life-style choices bombarding our subconscious minds from television advertising, we are literally hooked on all kinds of things. I am of the belief there is no way around it. We all tend to overdo and often forget the old adage, 'all things in moderation.' I myself love coffee. I only drink two cups a day, but I can assure you I don't function quite right without it. Certainly there are worse things, and I don't consume an entire pot in one sitting, but to a degree, I am hooked.

***

Shelley Kaehr, Ph.D.

At any given time, there is always some scientist doing a study about your favorite food or drink. While one study says it's the most horrible thing you could ever do to yourself, others claim your substance of choice is not only healthy, but may indeed be the cure to disease and the best single thing since the invention of sliced bread! I'm sure you know what I mean.

Coffee, for example, is cursed by many (probably green tea manufacturers) while at the same time, National Geographic did an article on it saying it actually stimulates brain function in small doses. Edgar Cayce, the world's greatest psychic, claimed coffee to be the number one antioxidant consumed by Americans. Personally, if it was good enough for the Aztecs, it's good enough for me!

The point is, we all have something we love, so whatever it is you love, its okay in moderation. If it's getting a bit out of control, threatening your mind or lessening enjoyment of some other part of your life, perhaps Amethyst can help you to bring the energy of peace and balance back into your reality.

TOP TEN

In addition, Amethyst will assist you in raising your overall vibrational frequency which will bring all sorts of residual benefits. When you raise or change frequency, your whole reality shifts.

The Purple Ray has a higher vibration than other colors so it assists in moving blockages and gently raising your frequency which is why it is in Top Ten as one of the most important healing stones ever.

These days our world is spinning so fast we cannot hold on to anything without pain. Amethyst will assist you in gracefully letting go, quite a lofty endeavor, and prepare you for rapid change for the better.

FOOD FOR THOUGHT

Did you know if you
heat amethyst either
artificially or in sunlight
it will become the golden
citrine stone? A new gem
that melds both of these
into one is called
Ametrine

7 – Citrine

Chemical Composition: SiO2
Located In: S. America, USA, Europe
Metaphysical Properties: Brings user
prosperity in the form of cash
Physical Healing: relieves stomach
aches

Like Amethyst, Citrine is also
of the quartz variety, getting its
golden yellow color from trace
amounts of iron, it is the sister stone
to Amethyst. Naturally forming
citrine is extremely rare. Most of
these pieces are artificially heat
treated and some gem enthusiasts
may think this diminishes its value,
but I disagree. However it arrives at
its golden state, the frequency of
this stone is extremely high and
unusually profound for those who use
it.

TOP TEN

If you saw the new Indiana Jones flick, *Kingdom of the Crystal Skulls*, you may recall the alien beings at the end of the movie had crystal skulls. Aside from the fact I think Spielberg is way ahead of his time, there may be some truth to that information, wherever it floated in from. If we are evolving to a new higher consciousness and if you consider silicon is the primary 'ingredient' in crystal, I believe the stones may be reaching more mass consciousness at this time to assist us in activating our silicon aspects in our dormant DNA in preparation for planetary shifts in consciousness.

I hope this makes sense...if not, email me! It's kind of a mind-boggling concept, but what I mean is that if we know we as a species are only using a fraction of our potential, it makes sense that by strengthening our current existing DNA and activating the strands we've identified as dormant, we automatically evolve by doing so. Crystals help people do that and from what I've seen, more and more people are suddenly having stones and minerals pop up on their spiritual radar screens.

***

Earlier in the book I described care and cleaning of gems and why it is necessary to do that from time to time because stones pick up on our energy and can get bogged down with it over time. Unlike most other stones, Citrine is special because it is one of only three I know of that does not require any kind of cleaning to remain in a pure and functional state. (In case you're wondering, the other two are kyanite and selenite, both featured prominently in my other book *Gemstone Journeys*).

This is significant because for some reason, citrine is not affected by our reacting to it and is therefore pure and clear to open energy centers and do all kinds of clearing on physical, mental/emotional, and spiritual levels in the energy bodies described in Part One of the book. Where normal stones would need to be taken outside, bathed in salt or smudged with a sage wand after awhile, citrine doesn't ever need to be, although its still nice to do it from time to time anyway. Why? Because our conscious mind enjoys ritual and I think it helps us to feel connected with the stones when we care for them in this way.

***

TOP TEN

When I'm working with people in hypnotherapy for example, I always bring a golden ball of protective light into their consciousness to surround and protect the physical body. Citrine is the physical manifestation of the golden ray, which is a beautifully healing and protective energy. Whether you use the citrine or simply evoke the golden light to swirl around you, it offers a protective shield for the physical, mental, emotional and spiritual self unlike any other. It brings feelings of safety and peace to everyone who I've worked with, probably because of this golden light.

It is especially attuned to our ability to receive – whether that is money, material stuff or just general flow and abundance. In healing I've used it to help clear the emotional body which is where our ability to create is found. When that energy field is clear, the person can create anything from art to wealth to positive flow in life. Citrine helps you release fears tied to lack and poverty consciousness, fear of success and self- sabotaging behaviors and limiting belief patterns that hold you back from having all you can and all you deserve.

Citrine has long been known as the Merchant's Stone and when left in store cash registers, the till begins to overflow. Likewise, people I know carry it in the wallet or purse for the same reason. Sales people dealing with the public would be well advised to cleanse their energy fields with Citrine before making sales calls because it changes the person's energy so as to attract financial abundance and sales. Really any business person or anyone who needs to bring an influx of funding into their reality would benefit from the stone. It raises your frequency, opens the chakras and other energy centers and allows you to be in a posture to receive. If cash is what you need, Citrine will energize and refresh you so you will be a money magnet!

In order to be successful, you can certainly use this stone, but you must also take action in order to make things happen. Allow me to elaborate...

Recently I received a call from a man who bought Citrine from me in hopes of making more money. He complained the stones weren't working, and questioned about it, said he just lost his job.

TOP TEN

"Did you look in the want ads?" I asked.

"No," he answered.

If you were a fly on the wall for this conversation, you would have seen me roll my eyes, sigh and shake my head. My goodness! This makes no sense whatsoever! Sometimes people need to *Get Real*, as Dr. Phil would say.

Let's face it - God Almighty is not going to strike a bolt of lightning through your living room tonight with a little package attached to it containing your heart's desire! Yes, I believe in the Law of Attraction and all of that, but in order to attract you must ACT! I think somewhere along the way people forgot that critical step to achieving all you want in life. No matter how positive your thoughts, at some point, you must get out there and take an action in order to make things happen in your life! It is as simple as that! This idea that things are arriving on a silver platter really drives me bananas!

It's about taking responsibility for your life and part of that means taking action. I was completely beside myself after this phone call, as you can imagine!

I believe all things are possible on earth. No matter how dire your circumstances are today, no matter your health, financial status, relationship status, you can absolutely turn your entire life around, change everything with proper thinking and change, but action is always required.

So yes, while Citrine stones create a frequency to assist you with your intentions, you must **do** something in order to get the results. Take action and use this stone as the focal point for your intention, meaning when you look at the stone, rub it while it is in your pocket or whatever, think of your desired outcome and then go out and take steps toward what you are trying to create.

As time continues to speed up, our thoughts are becoming things far more quickly than they used to and because of that you must be careful to monitor what you think. Thought combined with action, even small action, will yield results. Please remember to take action!

FOOD FOR THOUGHT
All green stones assist physical
healing and pain relief.

TOP TEN

6 – Aventurine

Chemical Composition: SiO2
Located In; S. Africa, India, Germany,
Austria, Arkansas, USA
Metaphysical Properties: Brings
material wealth and abundance
Physical Healing: alleviates aches and
pains, particularly back ache

Aventurine is another silicon
based quartz family stone...surprised?
Don't be! It appears in several colors
– green, yellow and red, mixed with
tiny gold flecks of iron pyrite which
assist you in healing the higher mind
and emotional body we discussed in
the earlier chapter.
The yellow and red varieties are
colored by Hematite, the other Top
Ten stone mentioned earlier, so they
carry an extra grounding energy.
Right now I'm working with some
really neat red pieces from India.

The kind I like best, though, is the green Aventurine which gets its color from a mica flecked stone called Fuchsite. I also like the green because of its ties to the heart chakra and the color of money.

Aventurine will help you with all of these things. Remember that any green stone assists the body in physical healing, and Aventurine is no exception. When I speak of physical healing, a lot of times the green stones help with pains, and Aventurine works great for the back.

Your emotional body is often tied to physical pain in the back which is a result of not feeling supported. If this is troublesome to you, work on that and it will help you. Aventurine will help you overcome that pain and move into a state of balance.

Have you ever reached the end of the day so worn out your body hurt when you went to bed just from lying there? It happened to me long ago, and I used Aventurine to help, and believe me, it did! As a side benefit, my business increased because its frequency is tied to abundance and prosperity.

***

TOP TEN

Aventurine is a great stone for carrying in the pocket throughout the day because it carries a frequency that allows you to receive what you need in life in the way of material goods, or the feeling of prosperity that comes with having all you need.

The gold flecks raise the frequency and connect you with higher realms where your prayers for peace, abundance and prosperity will be heard whether you speak them consciously or not. You might have noticed the Chinese and how they use the stone Jade for carvings and feng shui implements. Aventurine is sometimes known as Indian Jade because like pure jade, it brings an energy of abundance which is enhanced by the gold flecks in the stone.

It's a completely different energy from Citrine, though. Citrine reminds me of cash money, while Aventurine is more an abundance stone, meaning I have all I need and then some...

Try it! It works!

FOOD FOR THOUGHT

Colorado USA boasts sodalite as one of their major mineral deposits

5 – Sodalite

Chemical Comp. $Na_8Al_6Si_6O_{24}Cl_2$
Located In: Brazil, Colorado
Metaphysical Properties: brings balance, allows you to speak your truth by gently opening the throat
Physical Healing: tempers thyroid and hypoglycemic conditions

There are a lot of reasons why I put Sodalite on my list of Top Ten. With the unbelievably poor diet we're on these days, I think it's necessary for every medicine bag out there!
Sodalite specifically deals with the issues surrounding our thyroids and the way our bodies process sugars. Named for sodium content, this stone will help you bring balance to the delicate chemical systems of the body. In particular, it helps regulate the thyroid and the glucose and sugar production in the body.

TOP TEN

These days it is practically impossible to get the fructose corn syrup out of our systems because it is in nearly every food out there.

Without incredible diligence, I am convinced this will be around for awhile. I happen to believe the kids being born today will evolve and learn to operate on this stuff, but for the rest of us, Sodalite can help balance our systems and keep us going.

Any condition such as diabetes, hypoglycemia, etc. will benefit from this stone. I used it myself with great success to ward off fluctuations in my blood sugar years ago. I was having these episodes of crashing between meals and was told to try putting Sodalite on the space above my collar bone for awhile and sure enough, it balanced me out.

That combined with learning to eat several small meals throughout the day turned this condition around for me and I am so glad it did!

These type of health concerns are nearing epidemic proportions if they're not there already and something must be done about it! Meanwhile, try Sodalite!

Sodalite is dark blue with white calcium bands so it is also helpful for easing your stomach and building bone density. Calcium in any mineral offers similar healing support as a vitamin supplement.

The blue color resonates with the throat chakra which is another reason why it helps the thyroid which is located in that area of the body.

It has an extremely gentle and peaceful energy and can also be used to assist those who have trouble sleeping. Blue colors are always associated with emotional peace, healing and relaxation, so if you're stressed out a lot at work, or from other societal pressures, try carrying Sodalite with you in your pocket and see if things smooth out for you. I believe they will!

Some people report Sodalite helps with sleep. Again the peaceful blue and the calming influences of calcium act to relax you for a good night's rest.

FOOD FOR THOUGHT
Psychic Edgar Cayce mentioned
three kinds of Lapis in the life readings
scholars believe are Lapis Lazuli,
Malachite and Azurite

TOP TEN

4 – Lapis

Chemical Comp:
(Na,Ca)8(SiO4,S,CI)2I(AlSi)4l6
Located In: Afghanistan, Chile
Metaphysical Properties: psychic development, spiritually uplifting, reconnects you to Egyptian past lives
Physical Healing: relieves migraines and acid reflux

One of the most mystical stones on our planet, Lapis, has ties to the ancient world, Biblical times, and spiritual enlightenment.

Edgar Cayce, the world's greatest psychic, brought Lapis to prominence after mentioning it more than any other stone in his life readings, siting the stone as a great spiritual awakener and energetic support to those who once lived in ancient Egypt in past lives.

Like Aventurine, Lapis has flecks of gold mica which serve as transmitters of this ancient knowledge and remembrance.

Medicinally, Lapis is an incredibly powerful stone. It helps the stomach with acid reflux and aids in migraine headaches. I discovered this accidentally when a man bought a small piece of Lapis from me and wore it in his bandana (this was in Texas, of course! ha ha). Later he reported miraculous disappearance of his chronic migraines and acid reflux which are both related to each other. While writing *Edgar Cayce's Guide to Gemstones* I found a reference Cayce made in a reading where he noted the connection between the stomach and the migraine. I think it makes sense that if the stomach was too acidic, acid travels up the esophagus and could potentially cause a headache. So if you are suffering from either of these two conditions, or know someone who is, treat your acid reflux problem and you may find the other goes away as a by-product, and try carrying Lapis with you or wearing it as a necklace. It's worth a shot, I always say. Anything is better than medicines when you can avoid it.

TOP TEN

Over the years, I've seen many people try this and they found it works.

Between its ties to the ancient world and many Biblical sites, you cannot help but tune into those energies and times long ago when you use Lapis, opening yourself up to new levels of spiritual life. It is a powerful stone!

I wonder if people are now avoiding Lapis these days due to the increasing turmoil in the Middle East, where most of the world's production of this stone is found. I believe Lapis can assist you in connecting with those energies in order to offer prayer and support in hopes of a peaceful and amicable solution to the problems there.

While nothing has been settled concerning the Gaza area and Holy Land, there is always hope for brighter days and Lapis will help you direct much needed prayer to this part of the world.

FOOD FOR THOUGHT
Need Help in School?
Flourite helps you retain
information and make good grades!

3 – Fluorite

Chemical Composition: CaF_2
Located In: England, France, Mexico,
Colorado & Nevada, USA, Brazil
Metaphysical Properties: Helps you
concentrate and get work done
Physical Healing: assists eyesight and
relieves allergies

I have a special affinity in my
heart for the Fluorite stone, primarily
because it is the very first stone I
ever worked with and recognized its
incredible energy. In *Gemstone
Journeys* I told the story of the
shaman I met who placed a piece of
green Fluorite on my head and within
moments, I had an epiphany about
minerals that changed my life forever.
The Fluorite comes in three
colors – green, deep purple or clear.
You are attracted to different colors of
the stone for different reasons.

TOP TEN

The green ones help the heart, and throat area, the purple with the third eye energies.

Fluorite is significant among other reasons for the fact that it forms in crystals that are octahedron shaped, the same shape used to form the Great Pyramid at Giza. It is made of calcium – the most common element on earth, and fluoride, both known to strengthen and protect the teeth.

Fluorite energetically assists teeth and is also beneficial to your eyesight. I've used it myself for that purpose. If your eyes are strained from too much computer use, reading or working, put the round tumbled pieces on the eyes while you lay down for a brief nap. The energy of the stones assist your eyes in healing and when you wake up in twenty minutes or so, you will feel rested and refreshed.

I think this stone helped me ward off needing to wear glasses for years. Now I wear them primarily because I am in several writing groups and glasses are quite in vogue there. I feel sure I could restore my vision to its old glory by working with fluorite again!

Fluorite is a super for students. It's frequency helps you concentrate on what you read, allowing you to understand it and retain the information which can be particularly useful when taking tests. Years ago when I was in college, I was too busy goofing around to care about grades so I was an average student at best. When I returned to school in adulthood, two things helped me: hypnotherapy training and Fluorite.

I learned to put myself into trance prior to class so information the professor talked about would go straight into my subconscious mind where I could recall it later. What a revelation that was!

I would often get sleepy while studying and when I used Fluorite on my eyes, I would nap and wake up feeling refreshed and ready to go. That is how I accidentally discovered Fluorite helps allergies. When I put it on my eyes during my naps, several times I felt my sinuses clear.

Since traveling around speaking on the topic for years now, many students have also reported a positive effect while using the stone for allergens.

***

TOP TEN

Lately our brains are being bombarded by external stimuli and when that happens, the brain requires greater amounts of fuel to run. No wonder we have record numbers of people diagnosed with conditions such as ADHD. I believe we're being overloaded big time.

I joke about my own hyperactive behavior and how I temper it with exercise. Morning exercise helps me sit still and write in the afternoon. If you watched swimmer Michael Phelps in the Olympics, his mother reported the swimming pool provided his only outlet for burning off excess energy. On some level, I understand why this helped him...

Humanity is evolving. As we continue to expand ourselves, kids today are smarter than us and need to be challenged. Unfortunately, the current ill-equipped educational system is sorely behind. Please, don't get me started on this!

Fluorite assists ADHD and brings focus and concentration to those who need it.

2 – Serpentine

Chemical Composition: $H_2Mg_2Si_2O_2$
Located In: England, China, New Zealand
Metaphysical Properties: Teaches you are a spirit having physical experience
Physical Healing Properties: Pain relief & healing for cancers, AIDS, arthritis, Fibromyalgia, back aches – anyone in extreme pain will benefit!

In my other books I report on the miraculous healings from Serpentine users and discovered it may be because it is a magnesium-based stone. Several people reported the stone turning black, taking on their illness and I spent a lot of time wondering why and how this was happening.

***

TOP TEN

Magnesium is the key ingredient in Epsom salts which I've been touting for years as not only helping people in pain, but can be used with great results as a way to clear unwanted influences around us. Use it in a hot bath to pull toxins from the body and cleanse your energy field!

As for Serpentine, a scientist once told me the stone is reacting with the skin somehow, and after much research I discovered Serpentine is definitely absorbing the excess acid in the skin.

Our diets are filled with so many artificial ingredients, food colors, dyes and preservatives that we are becoming too acidic. Acid and alkaline imbalances have been theoretically linked to cancers and all kinds of disease.

A friend of mine said once she straightened out her acid alkaline balance, her cancer disappeared. Not surprising!

Further, I would say magnesium supplements are important for our health, and chiropractors I've talked to through the years claim we are not getting enough in our diet.

***

I started buying regular over-the-counter magnesium zinc tablets years ago and take two before bedtime with a calcium citrate vitamin. They help me relax and sleep, and I also believe they assist my body in balancing the alkaline within.

We are a society out of balance and we have to get back on track in a lot of ways. This internal balance of the body represents the fact that our beings are merely a complex set of chemical reactions and we are quite delicate and must take care to keep everything in check and in balance.

Serpentine may hold the key vibrationally to help us get ourselves back in alignment so our bodies can heal naturally and that is why it is the number two of the top ten. It takes on your illness, absorbs it and helps you heal.

FOOD FOR THOUGHT

Magnesium Sulfide also known as Epsom Salt, is a powerful cleanser for your energy field. The two other kinds of salt are sea salt, and table salt, sodium chloride, which is great for protecting the energy around your property.

TOP TEN

1 – Bloodstone

Chemical Composition: SiO_2
Located In: Brazil, China, throughout the USA
Metaphysical Properties: Christ Consciousness
Physical Healing: lungs, heart, circulation – any serious conditions will be helped by this stone

I've been asked how I could choose one stone as the "best" and why in the world the Bloodstone would be my choice of all the mineral kingdom has to offer.

I don't believe Bloodstone is necessarily "better" than other stones, but it was the first stone to show me in physical reality that something happened. Once I saw it turn from dark green to clear white years ago, I was instantly a believer!

Normally colored dark green with red flecks (Hematite), I was told the red will be absorbed by the body, but what I saw was all color get zapped from it, a phenomenon that continues to baffle my mind.

Since that first encounter, I've recommended Bloodstone hundreds of times for critically ill people and have continued to see positive results again and again, including the following:

The stone on the cover was used by a man who had a plethora of illnesses (more on him later in the book) including congestive heart failure. After carrying Bloodstone in his front shirt pocket a week later no evidence of it could be found.

Another friend had family members with leukemia who are now in remission after using Bloodstone, and following doctor's treatment.

A police officer told me his mother once gave him a bag of stones and made him promise to carry them always. He never opened the bag but put it in his pocket. One night during a dangerous raid, the bag ripped open, exposing a piece of Lapis, a cracked piece of Hematite, Rose Quartz and a Bloodstone turned completely white!

TOP TEN

Spiritually speaking, I am compelled to believe Bloodstone truly carries the frequency of Christ Consciousness. When you think of the life of Christ, the sacrifice He made to humanity, Bloodstones sacrifice by allowing us to take on their physical attributes to heal.

***

Chemically speaking, Bloodstone is identical to quartz although it is in the family of minerals called Chalcedony. Carnelian, carrier of the Orange Ray, is also in this mineral family.

Bloodstone is still sometimes referred to by its Greek name, *heliotrope*, meaning 'sun turner'.

I did some experimenting on this to see if the sun turns the stone, and noticed a piece in my window sill gained more red spots after direct light exposure. That is the iron content reacting to light, although I don't know what it means yet in terms of healing potential.

The green in Bloodstone is due to an element called Chlorite which I believe has amazing healing properties.

Shelley Kaehr, Ph.D.

In the healing community right now there is a neat stone called Chlorite Quartz. Chlorite is an element in the periodic table, so it is like a dust, a trace mineral. In these quartz specimens, the Chlorite looks like somebody blew some dark green dust through the clear stone. It is really neat.

Recently after Coast to Coast, I was contacted by a concerned father of a little girl suffering from Cystic Fibrosis which is a serious condition of the lungs. He wrote to ask me what stone I recommended for his daughter and although I had not had any pieces of Chlorite in at the time, I instantly saw a piece flash in my mind's eye. Later I learned this is the element in Bloodstone and I remembered the first time the stone turned white was with a client of mine with lung problems. What is the connection? I don't know for sure, but I am inclined to think on the physical level the chlorite along with the detoxifying properties from Hematite are what makes the Bloodstone so powerful.

As I continue to learn more and receive more feedback from people, I will let you know!

TOP TEN

My Bloodstone Story

I have a friend who is a world renowned author. Years ago we traveled together for lectures, and were invited to work with a family who was suffering from deaths of two close family members. I do not want to go into specifics, other than to say it was an incredibly disturbing situation and they needed counseling.

Right before I left town, I was guided to pick up my very favorite piece of raw bloodstone. By *raw* I mean it was big with rough edges, not polished. It was a gorgeous dark green piece I got from a friend and although I loved it, I never worked with it before.

I put the stone in my pocket and forgot about it. On Sunday evening, I unpacked, happened to find it, and when I looked, the Bloodstone was mustard yellow color!!! I couldn't believe it and assumed it was offering me protection from an unavoidably negative situation. Once again, I was a believer.

So without being too analytical, whatever the reason it works, let's all be glad and take it on faith as a miraculous example of the mineral kingdom's power to change our lives.

PART THREE

Healing with
TOP TEN

TOP TEN

Now What?
How to Use Stones in Healing

Healing Self First

We are taught to do for others before ourselves. This is a nice concept in theory but on some level it doesn't work because if you run out of steam, you can't possibly help anyone else.

Stone healing is like this. I think it's a good idea to do this first for yourself and then try it on others. First because you need to rejuvenate before working on someone else, and also by doing so, you learn about the stones and can pass this enthusiasm on to others.

In self healing you simply get whichever stones you are guided to use and lay down. Place the stones either over your chakra centers or any place that feels like it needs energy.

Now go to sleep, or zone out, for about twenty minutes or so. At first, if you're like me, you won't feel a thing, then all of a sudden you will feel a rush of energy. I think this is the body reacting to the wave of energy emitted from the stone.

Normally it takes about twenty minutes and then that rush will stop and you will open your eyes. I use stones a lot when I go to bed at night. I lay them around my stomach and heart so the vibrations can move through my body.

Sometimes the energy is so strong, it feels like I am being magnetized and cannot move. About this time, I drift off to sleep and sometimes have visions.

Recently I was meditating with a piece of Shamanite which is a new stone found in only one place in the world. It comes from a sacred Native American ceremonial site and the people must be blindfolded when taken to it. It has incredible power and energy and when I put it on my stomach, I had a bright and clear vision of a warrior in face paint. It was more than a dream, much clearer and really profound. I still don't know what it means exactly, but the stone gave me a lot of energy!

TOP TEN

After this dreamlike state is finished, if you're like me, you will know when you are done receiving the healing and energy from the stone because the energy release will taper off and you will find yourself opening your eyes, coming back into the room.

Even at night, I find I am wide awake again so I put the stone to one side, still keeping it in my bed normally, and I roll over and drift off to sleep.

I used to take a lot of naps in the afternoon, and this is another great time to try this, particularly if you get sleepy like I do. Try it and you will find yourself feeling refreshed and energized for the evening.

Healing for Others

Once you try this yourself, you can do healings for others by having them lay flat on the floor, bed, or massage table. Pick stones that "speak" to you and lay them on the person, on the heart, stomach, neck.

Do not analyze this too much. There is no right or wrong way to do this! You are much more in tuned with this than you realize so just do what feels right to you and go for it! You will always do the right thing! I promise!

After you place your stones on the person's body, begin sending energy, such as Reiki. If you are not formally trained in energy healing modalities, you can still send energy to the person by putting your hands over the body and running your hands through the person's energy field while sending them positive intentions such as peace, love, healing, joy, relaxation, or anything else you think they need.

When you pray for someone, you send well wishes and good intent. I'm sure you've heard all about folks having miraculous recoveries from illness and despair after the entire congregation got together to pray for them, right? This is the same thing, and believe me, it works! When you send positive energy to people, they feel and appreciate it.

If you are a massage therapist, use the stones in combination with massage. You probably heard of hot stone massages. They are amazing and this works the same way, only using different stones.

Experiment with this, have some fun and see what happens!

TOP TEN

About the Stone on the Cover
Conclusion

The stone on the cover of this book is unusual. Most bloodstones, including the ones I've seen provide most miraculous healings, are very dark green with tiny red specks.

My late friend Joe used the bright red stone on the cover with some success despite the fact he was literally a walking medical condition during the time I knew him. He was diabetic, had congestive heart failure, renal failure, and came to me several times for energy balancing. During his last few years on earth he used bloodstone and swore by it.

You're probably asking if it works so well, what happened to him? Why is he still not alive and kicking? Aside from obvious reasons that neither you or I will make it out of this place alive, the question brings up another fundamental you must understand when working with this or any other kind of vibrational healing method. Basically put, neither you nor I are God. We have no control over life and death matters. The role as healer is to be conduit for energy, without judgment and attachment, which is easier said than done.

Why one person gets up and gets well and another doesn't is one of the most frustrating and simultaneously fascinating aspects of this work. I had to learn long ago what someone else does or does not do in regards to their own personal healing journey is none of my business. That sounds harsh, I know, but it's true. Medical doctors face this hourly in their work. Their job is to save lives, yet sometimes that isn't possible.

There is a time to live and a time to die. I do not know when that time is any more than you do. I believe that these mineral gifts can provide you with the necessary frequency shifts to enhance your well being, but beyond that, I do not have the answers. Nobody does. We won't until we check out of planet earth.

TOP TEN

In any kind of healing, there is always the question of *healing ethics*, meaning, is it okay for me to send healing to you if I don't ask permission first?

This is complicated. I don't think you can walk up to somebody and ask if they *want* healing. If you do, they will say yes or no, but that is not necessarily a reflection of what they really want or need. Only the soul knows what it needs, and that is not something that any person can consciously answer.

Years ago when I had my radio show on KLIF in Dallas, a woman contacted me, desperate to help her son who was dying of cancer.

When I showed up to do some energy work on him, nothing happened. My hands were cold as ice cubes, and just as I was about to say something to him and his mother, he appeared in my mind's eye and told me he did not want to be healed.

Sure enough, within a couple weeks, he passed. His mother wrote to me recently to say she finally understands he is at peace, and it was what he wanted, despite all her attempts to save him. That story and man will stay in my mind forever...

Similarly, I volunteered for a hospice years ago, which was one of the most emotionally difficult challenges I ever experienced.

There was a sweet lady I took care of who we called "mom." Mom had Super-Nuclear Palsy, a nervous system disorder. She was completely immobile, but could speak by raising one finger for yes, two for no.

During out time together, I noticed my hands would never get warm, no healing, other than companionship was ever administered, because her goal in hospice was to transition from this plane to the next.

I experimented with this once, tried to concentrate to see if my hands could send her energy. They couldn't.

Always remember it isn't you doing the healing, it is from a higher power. You have no control over life or death matters, either.

I feel compelled to share this with anyone who is seriously considering healing work. There is no way to beat death. The best thing you can do for a loved one is to be okay with where they are on their path, even when it isn't what you want.

TOP TEN

You are an energetic spiritual being. Your physical body is only one part of the equation of YOU.

When you begin to understand energetic and spiritual imbalances appear long before physical symptoms, when you understand you are more than your body, you begin to see the world through new eyes and have new opportunities for peace and wellness in your life.

Recently I've noticed more and more people experiencing what I did years ago – they are sick, tired, desperate for new answers to old questions. Alternative therapies are quickly rising in popularity and will hopefully continue to become more prevalent in the future.

Regardless of how you use this information, I hope it opened your eyes and mind to all mother nature has available for you, and I wish you peace, joy, healing and happiness on your journey in life.

Shelley Kaehr, Ph.D.

WE are The Ones

We've been waiting for...

-Unknown Hopi Elder

TOP TEN

Bibliography

Berggren, Karen. *Circle of Shaman: Healing Through Ecstasy, Rhythm & Myth*, Destiny Books, 1998.

Bridges, Carol. *The Medicine Woman Inner Guidebook*, US Games, Inc., 1987.

Broomfield, John. *Other Ways of Knowing: Recharting Our Future with Ageless Wisdom*, Inner Traditions, 1997.

Doreal. *The Emerald Tablets of Thoth the Atlantean*, Brotherhood of the White Temple, 1992.

Dunne, J.W. *An Experiment with Time*, Hampton Roads, 2001.

Endredy, James. *Beyond 2012: A Shaman's Call to Personal Change and the Transformation of Global Consciousness*, Llewellyn, 2008.

Essene, Virginia. *New Cells, New Bodies, NEW LIFE!* Spiritual Education Endeavors, 1991.

Feather, Ken Eagle. *Toltec Dreaming: Don Juan's Teachings on the Energy Body*, Bear & Co., 2007.

Flem-Ath, Rand and Colin Wilson. *The Atlantis Blueprint: Unlocking the Mystery of a Long-lost Civilization*, Time Warner Books, 2000.

Goldman, Jonathan. *The 7 Secrets of Sound Healing*, Hay House, 2008.

Hogue, John. *Nostradamus: The Complete Prophecies*, Element Books, Ltd, 1997.

Ingalls, Arthur. *How to Heal Yourself Spiritually*, Crosing Publishing Company, 1998.

Jenkins, John Major. *Unlocking the Secrets of 2012: Galactic Wisdom of the Ancient Skywatchers*, Sounds True, 2007.

Kenyon, J. Douglas. *Forbidden Science: From Ancient Technologies to Free Energy*, Bear & Co, 2008.

TOP TEN

Markham, Ursula. *Fortune-Telling by Crystals and Semi-Precious Stones: A Practical Guide to Their Use in Divination, Meditation and Healing*, The Aquarian Press, 1987.

Meadows Kenneth. *Shamanic Spirit: A Practical Guide to Personal Fulfillment*, Bear & Co., 1995.

Mitchell, John. *Secrets of the Stones: New Revelations of Astro-archaeology and the Mystical Sciences of Antiquity*, Inner Traditions, 1989.

Nabokov, Peter. *Where the Lightning Strikes: The Lives of American Indian Sacred Places*, Penguin Books, 2006.

Naydler, Jeremy. *Shamanic Wisdom in the Pyramid Texts: Mystical Tradition of Ancient Egypt*, Inner Traditions, 2005.

Rael, Joseph and Mary Elizabeth Marlow. *Being and Vibration*, Council Oak Books, 1993.

Ross, Dr. A.C. Ehanamani. *Mitakuye Oyasin: We are All Related*, Wico'ni Waste', 1989.

Schumann, Walter. *Gemstones of the World*, Simon & Schuster, 1997.

Snow, Chet. *Mass Dreams of the Future: Do we face an apocalypse or a global spiritual awakening? The choice is ours*. Deep Forest Press: 1989.

Star, Nancy Red. *Legends of the Star Ancestors: Stories of Extraterrestrial Contact from Wisdom Keepers Around the World*, Bear & Company, 2002.

Stewart, Iris, J. *Sacred Woman, Sacred Dance: Awakening Spirituality Through Movement and Ritual*, Inner Traditions, 2000.

Stewart, R. J. *The Spiritual Dimension of Music: Altering Consciousness for Inner Development*, Destiny Books, 1987.

Toth, Max. Pyramid *Prophecies: The Timeless Message of Sacred Stones Reveals Our Future*, Destiny Books, 1979.

About the Author

Shelley Kaehr, Ph.D. is author of over fifteen nonfiction books on the mind-body connection. She is a featured expert in the media on a wide variety of paranormal and alternative healing subjects, and most loves sharing her expertise on the healing powers of gems and minerals.

She is widely known for her work in the field of past-life regression and parallel universes, her work in consciousness is endorsed by the greatest thinkers of our time.

Shelley's first two romance novels, *Kiss at Blarney Castle* and *Road to Casablanca* by Leah Leonard are now available on Amazon.com, and her murder mystery *Deep Currency* by Annette Shelley (featuring Detective Mario Martinez) will be released in summer 2009.

Shelley has two new nonfiction titles coming in 2009: *The Life You Deserve*, based on years of research assisting people in finding their passion, and *Damned: True Tales of the Cursed, Hexed and Bewitched,* written after Shelley received dozens of letters from people claiming to be cursed. The book talks about the connection of mind and body in the creation of reality and how people can turn their lives around by simply changing their thoughts.

Shelley lives near Dallas, Texas.

Visit her online:
www.shelleykaehr.com
www.leahleonard.com
www.annetteshelley.com

CPSIA information can be obtained at www.ICGtesting.com
Printed in the USA
BVOW081519140912

300309BV00006B/1/P